BEYOND DIFFERENCES: THE ART OF COLLABORATIVE PARENTING

Christina Wade Perrone, J.D.

Jacobs & Whitehall
21750 Hardy Oak Blvd
Suite 104 – 51700
San Antonio, Texas 78258
(888) 570-7338
www.jacobsandwhitehall.com

Ordering Information:

Quantity sales. Special discounts are available on quantity purchases by corporations, associations, and others. For details, contact the publisher at the address above.

Orders by U.S. trade bookstores and wholesalers. Please contact Jacobs & Whitehall: Tel: (888) 991-2766 or visit www.jacobsandwhitehall.com.

Printed in the United States of America

Published in 2024

DISCLAIMER

This publication is intended to be used for educational purposes only. No legal advice is being given, and no attorney-client relationship is intended to be created by reading this material. The author assumes no liability for any errors or omissions or for how this book or its contents are used or interpreted, or for any consequences resulting directly or indirectly from the use of this book. For legal or any other advice, please consult an experienced attorney or the appropriate expert, who is aware of the specific facts of your case and is knowledgeable in the law in your jurisdiction.

The Perrone Law Firm, PLLC

2714 Washington Street, Box No. 146
Greenville, TX 75401
www.perronelawfirm.com
(903) 461-7388

TESTIMONIALS

"Ms. Perrone and her team are fierce and know the law in the areas they practice. They will represent your family like it is their own. They respond promptly and accurately to meet your needs. She is a pleasure to work with. We trust our family with her."

– Jeff W.

****

"5 stars all the way across. Super nice, personable, dependable, thorough, detail oriented; gets the job done!"

– Karla S.

****

"This is an amazing law firm. Ms. Perrone goes above and beyond for her clients. We had an awesome adoption because of her, have remained friends and she always answer my questions."

– Crystal M.

****

"Christina Perrone is knowledgeable and passionate about her work and those she represents! She is second to none."

– Anne Marie, R.

****

"The BEST attorney I've ever met! Most attorneys are not very personable if they are amazing at what they do! But she is by far the exception!"

– Regina S.

****

"Honest and reliable!! Best attorney around!"

– Kellye Sullivan-R.

****

"Did a GREAT JOB with the adoption! Everything went as planned with no surprises or unnecessary delays."

– Paul W.

****

"[Christina] is not only an excellent lawyer but also an amazing, caring and trustworthy person."

– Holly B.

****

"[Christina] is knowledgeable and passionate about her work. The attention to detail and care she has for each client is what makes her a Great attorney!"

– Kim B.

****

"Christina has been amazing with our case. She truly cares and has a gift of interacting with the children that make them love her. It shows she wants what's best for them!"

– Shelly M.

****

"Could not recommend a more giving and kind - hearted person. She knows her law and goes above and beyond to assist her clients!"

– Melissa D.

****

"Mrs. Perrone is great in her field. She does an Amazing job and loves children. I highly recommended her"

– Leslie W.

****

"Drive, hardworking and passionate about all that she does! This attorney is THE best."

– Jordan Floyd H.

****

"Christina Perrone is an outstanding attorney with a great passion for her work and clients. I highly recommend her."

– Samuel H.

****

"She is passionate, knowledgeable, and extremely helpful. All qualities that are important in a lawyer."

– Jaime W.

****

TABLE OF CONTENTS

ABOUT THE AUTHOR

I started the Perrone Law Firm in 2016, after almost a decade working in commercial litigation. While I enjoyed my career in commercial litigation, I eventually lost some of the passion that originally led me to pursue a career in law. I realized that my true calling was in helping families, and specifically in helping children.

This led me to make a complete switch from business litigation to child welfare and private family law cases. After learning much of the law while working for the State of Texas' child welfare system for a couple of years, I knew that the biggest difference I could make would be by opening my own firm. I began to specialize in sub-fields like divorce and custody disputes, child welfare litigation, and adoption. I represent children, parents, and caregivers in a variety of family law cases.

In 2021, I became a certified parenting facilitator, devoting a large portion of my time and legal resources to helping caregivers learn effective strategies in a variety of co-parenting relationships. A parenting facilitator is an attorney who works with parties - typically represented by their own counsel - in divorce or child custody litigation, specifically as to matters of co-parenting. As a parenting facilitator, I help parents and caregivers work together to create a sustainable, mutually agreeable parenting plan, focusing on the best interests of the children involved. Our goal is ultimately to establish a parenting plan that works for the family outside of the courtroom for years to come.

In fact, the whole premise behind parenting facilitation is to settle these cases outside of the courtroom. If successful, parenting facilitation resolves conflict between the parties without requiring the decision of a judge or jury. Instead of an arbitrary court decision that the parties then have to adhere to, parenting facilitation gives the parties a chance to work together to make an agreement they can all be happy with and agree to implement.

Through my work as a parenting facilitator, I focus on helping parents learn specific skills in how to co-parent their children, and to keep putting the children first. I help them zero in on the key issues and really encourage them to work together to develop agreements and parenting plans that will actually work in the real world. Ideally, this prevents families from having to continue to litigate in court year after year, attempting to modify or change court-ordered possession schedules and parenting plans.

I'm also certified as a Family Law and Child Welfare Mediator. As a certified mediator, if I'm not acting as a parenting facilitator or an attorney representing one of the parties, I am available to assist the parties reach a parenting solution through a mediated settlement agreement. Mediation can result in sound decision-making, lessening resentment, greater understanding, improved communication, and transformation of relationships. Mediation services also benefit families by avoiding costly and often hurtful litigation. As a family law mediator, I seek to promote discussion and negotiation that allows the participants involved to exchange divergent views, ask questions, discuss difficult topics and find solutions. The clients have control over the process to reach an agreement. These agreements then get taken to court and incorporated into a Final Order.

In addition, I have completed the necessary continuing legal education (CLE) hours to serve as an Amicus Attorney for children. This area of my practice is where my passion to serve is most notable. Often, when children are stuck in the middle of a pending custody case, the court will appoint an Amicus Attorney to work with the children and the parents or caregivers to help determine what is in the children's best interests. The Amicus Attorney then writes her recommendations, which are either given directly to the court or to the parties' attorneys to work towards a positive resolution.

An Amicus Attorney is crucial in safeguarding the child's rights and ensuring his or her needs are prioritized within the legal process. As an Amicus Attorney, I focus on understanding the facts behind the caregivers' disputes and how they affect the children they share. Removing emotion and bias, I use the facts to determine what is best for the child and how to minimize or eliminate any trauma to the child caused by having two homes.

In each of these four areas of practice, I am eager and determined to help parents and children going through the divorce or custody process.

Who Is This Book For And What Do You Want Your Readers To Gain From It?

I want this book to be used primarily by two different groups of people:

- Caregivers Learning to Co-Parent. Caregivers who are learning how to co-parent their children and maintain the health of their family through a divorce or separation are going to find a lot of successful tools in this book. I also want this book to teach them how to put the right focus on creating a healthy co-parenting relationship. Readers should be encouraged to focus on putting their children first and striking the best balance in a custody or parenting plan that helps their children thrive between two homes.

- Professionals Who Work With Co-Parents. I also wrote this book with professionals who work with co-parents in mind. This could include other family law or divorce attorneys, other parenting coordinators or facilitators, and counselors who work with both children and adults in these cases. Using this book as a guide to focus clients on key issues and making important decisions for families, professionals should find this book as a valuable resource to help clients achieve positive outcomes.

CHAPTER 1

WHAT IS CO-PARENTING?

Co-Parenting is a relationship between caregivers that should aim to facilitate cohesive and healthy parenting by both parties. The most effective co-parenting comes from the creation of a respectful partnership focused on the children of the relationship.

Children raised by co-parents have parents or caregivers that no longer live together in the same home. This means the children must learn to live between two different homes. Learning to divide a child's time between two homes and two caregivers is difficult but not impossible!

It is our hope and aim to focus adult custodial parties on caregiving for their children and on creating a relationship that's built on trust, with love and compassion for each of the individuals involved. Always strive to focus on the best interest of the children they are seeking to raise together.

It is a well-established fact that children from divorce or separation can struggle to become healthy, balanced, and productive adults. In my practice, I have met just about every version of a caregiver there is, and not much of anything surprises me at this point. The outcome of a child's wellbeing is much less dependent on the personality of the caregiver, than it is on how the caregivers overcome their differences and role model effective and positive relationships in front of their child.

What Does Bad Co-Parenting Look Like?

Bad co-parenting happens when the co-parenting relationship is dominated or disrupted by negative feelings, including distrust, anger, or resentment. Bad co-parenting loses its focus on the children and shifts towards the adults involved. Nearly 100% of parents would agree that they want what is best for their children. And while anger and emotions can cloud a parent's judgment, that soft spot for a child's well-being often presents the avenue to diffuse tension and focus on working together as a co-parent in a healthy way.

Angry, distant, volatile relationships lead to emotional and disruptive parenting styles when not checked. There are many ways that these feelings can find their way into the co-parenting relationship. Often, there are residual feelings of betrayal or distrust from an event that led to the dissolution of the marriage or romantic relationship. This dissolution – created by the occurrence of negative event – must now be used as the foundation to develop a co-parenting relationship that is positive, trusting, and encouraging.

It's understandable for co-parents to still feel anger or resentment in some way when it comes to their former significant other. This is especially true if there was a major betrayal or harmful act perpetrated by the former partner that led to the dissolution of the marriage/romantic relationship.

However, if you're bringing that anger, distrust, and resentment into the co-parenting dynamic, then that will very quickly lead to unsuccessful co-parenting. It is more important to lead the path that focuses on your children's well-being and future than it is to cast blame for past errors.

Additionally, co-parenting tends to become unsuccessful when co-parents are in competition with one another in unhelpful ways. For example, if one or both parents are focused more on ensuring that they have the most time with the children, or that the children have the most fun at their home, then that arrangement is likely to devolve into unsuccessful co-parenting.

Co-parenting that involves poor communication, lack of cooperation, and a failure to prioritize the well-being of the children disregards the emotional needs of the children involved. Including ongoing conflicts, inconsistent parenting strategies, and a disregard for the children's needs for a healthy environment will have negative effect on a child's mental and emotional health. This may cause the children to experience stress, anxiety, and instability as a result of their parents' strained relationship.

Therefore, I discourage any individual involved in co-parenting from allowing feelings of resentment, anger, and betrayal to dominate their co-parenting relationship. I would also encourage all co-parents to refrain from creating an environment based on competition, getting the most time with the children, or being "the fun house." Children are benefitted by their easy (and almost immediate) forgiveness response. Because of this, children are quickly able to realize that they need both of their parents – divorce or separation just simply places those parents in two separate homes. Learning to work with the other parent reaps many benefits for your children – not only for the present but for the future as well.

Chapter 2

Legal Guidelines For Shared Custody

Each state has a set of laws that help to define and detail a parent's rights and access to their children. In Texas, the laws that relate to a parent's time and rights to their children discuss a parent's conservatorship status, which is similar to the phrase "custody". It's a very common phrase in popular culture and is the phrase that people usually use to refer to the underlying concept. Just about everybody who calls a law office or walks into a courtroom uses the term "custody". Just today, I heard a client say, “I need to get a custody agreement quick! I'm fighting my husband for custody in this divorce.”

However, Texas law doesn't actually use the paradigm of “custody”. Instead, it specifically defines the rights to children between two parents or caregivers by appointing conservators of the children and specifying terms of possession and access.

Furthermore, in Texas, there are two types of conservatorship. It is important to understand the different rights afforded to parents, at least on a general level, to apply that knowledge to developing a positive co-parenting relationship. In co-parenting, effective collaboration and communication are essential, especially when sharing legal custody. A broad overview of two types of conservatorship, legal custody, in Texas are as follows:

a) Managing Conservatorship: Texas law presumes that both parents should be appointed joint managing conservators. Specific facts and circumstances must be proven to rebut that presumption.[1] The managing conservator will make all of the decisions about the children's daily living, focusing on what's best for the child. For instance, they decide matters about where they go to school, where they live as their primary residence, and the specifics of their invasive medical and dental care, psychological or psychiatric treatment, and educational circumstances. This status also gives the conservator power to grant or deny certain permissions, such as permission to marry or join the armed services before the age of 18. There are many other rights afforded to a managing conservator. When there are two parents or caregivers splitting the conservatorship, they are called joint managing conservators.

b) Possessory Conservatorship: Possessory conservators have a different set of rights and

[1] A court may consider several factors, like a history of domestic violence or child abuse, in overcoming the presumption that both parents should be appointed joint managing conservators.

responsibilities over a child. At the simplest level, possessory conservators have a right to receive information about their child that third parties would usually be barred from receiving. Possessory conservators may receive information from educational institutions, doctors' offices, psychologists, therapists, and counselors, for example. However, it is important to note that possessory conservators do not have the same ability to make decisions about a child's life as managing conservators.

Each conservator of the child has some rights at all times or when in possession of the child. These rights are primarily focused on receiving the information and duties to provide appropriate care and direct moral or religious upbringing. In essence, managing conservatorship involves decision-making, while possessory conservatorship is more about physical custody or visitation time with the children.

Parents will want to have a clear understanding of the custodial rights afforded to each parent in any co-parenting plan prior to formalizing the agreement; this is so that there is no confusion about future decision making abilities. It should also be clear by now that both parents or caregivers must work together to make decisions in the best interest of the children through cooperation and mutual respect. It is key to navigate these choices for the children ensuring that their welfare remains the top priority.

Does Co-Parenting Always Have To Involve A Legal Custody Agreement?

Co-parenting does not have to involve a custody agreement approved or ordered by a court. This is important for co-parents to know and is also important for non-legal professionals working with co-parents and children (i.e., counselors, therapists, etc.) to know. However, by not having an enforceable agreement, approved by a court, parents are limited in the actions they can take to ensure they receive the appropriate time with their children. Additionally, having a legal custody agreement for co-parents provides clarity, structure, and legal enforceability.

Going to court can be expensive, sometimes prohibitively so for many families. In many cases, it may be a number of months or even years before the parties can work with legal professionals to craft a court-ordered custody or possession arrangement. If that is the case, we want to focus on helping each individual caregiver work together to create a co-parenting relationship that fosters agreements prior to establishing a legally binding court order.

Ideally, we want to get to parties to the point where they are able to determine and agree on what is best for their children and implement those actions without costly litigation and courtroom battles. Formalizing the arrangement legally can then help prevent future disputes and ensure that both parents are on the same page for their children.

Problems often arise if one parent begins dating, or if one parent wants to move away and take the children. By establishing a court order when you are working well with your co-parent, you will ensure that you are more likely to reach an agreement that is focused on your child's best interests. The court order then helps prevent future disagreements. If major conflicts arise, caregivers will have an order in place that was agreed to when things were working in a more positive environment. It is important to remember that a court order is the minimum expected of both parents by outlining the rights and responsibilities of each parent, covering aspects like visitation schedules, decision-making authority, and child support.

CHAPTER 3

ISSUES THAT AFFECT NEW CO-PARENTING AT THE START OF THE DIVORCE OR SEPARATION

In most cases involving divorce or the end of a romantic relationship—especially in cases where there is a dispute regarding conservatorship of the children or child support, unsuccessful co-parenting strategies are a common occurrence. Some cases involve establishing a father's rights to the children (referred to as paternity) and the previously single mother is now faced with learning to parent her children with another parent for the benefit of the children.

These challenges can be overcome if the parties are willing to make the necessary changes. The most effective way to remedy the issues depends on the case, the co-parents, and the situation in question. However, general co-parenting education—either from the perspective of a legal professional or a counseling professional—incorporated into each caregiver's perspective of a custodial agreement sets the foundation for a successful co-parenting future. It may just be a matter of one or both parties needing a simple expansion of their perspective. Focusing the caregivers on the child's ability to thrive in their environments, and removing the mentality of just surviving this situation until it's no longer needed, allows for positive changes to grow.

Almost every case will begin with at least some level of co-parenting dysfunction. Caregivers need help to get on the right track. If, however, there's already a great co-parenting relationship, similar principles apply; it's not going to continue without a good deal of effort, work, and communication.

The ultimate goal, even when co-parenting relationships start out great, is to encourage the parents to use the skills and the strong foundation necessary to keep the co-parenting relationship successful in the future. All parents need to establish and use successful communication patterns so that if any conflicts ever arise, they can be handled effectively.

What Are Common Co-Parenting Pitfalls At The Beginning Of The Journey?

Many co-parents suffer from a lack of communication or a failure to communicate in a healthy manner as their relationships with one another are dissolving. Co-parents are encouraged to focus on communication with a purpose and clarity about the children to help eliminate the emotions associated with the romantic relationship that is ending. Communication focused on the children's needs prioritizes their well-being and keeps them protected from the emotional turmoil of the romantic relationship ending. This also means that co-parents should not use their children as messengers in lieu of communicating with the other parent.

Additionally, co-parents may discourage time with the children for the other co-parent. A better plan is to encourage co-parents to work together to create specific parenting schedules that focus on giving the children the freedom to spend time with and love both of their parents or caregivers. Children suffer greatly with the loss of a loved caregiver, and when that loss is intentionally caused by another caregiver the child loves, the impact is even more severe. All co-parents should strive to encourage their children to enjoy their time with each parent and be consistent and available upon the children's return to that home.

The third most common pitfall is related to negative talk about the other co-parent with the children. It is imperative, and part of many standing court orders, that co-parents refrain from speaking a derogatory manner about the children's other parent. Instead, co-parents should focus on using words that speak life and joy to the children about the other co-parent. Many times it is not enough to simply refrain from speaking negatively about your co-parent. Other body language like facial expressions and attitudes of disinterest can also be observed by even young children. As adults, it is important for co-parents to keep those behaviors in check and to go the extra step of speaking positively and with encouragement and support for the other co-parent.

All of these co-parenting pitfalls can be avoided by remembering that it is crucial to maintain open communication, establish consistent parenting strategies, and focus on the best interests of the children.

Is It Possible To Co-Parent Well During The Separation And Divorce Process, Or Does Co-Parenting Have To Be Handled After Divorce Or End Of The Romantic Relationship Is Finalized?

If you have children, you must think about and consider co-parenting at the initial onset of separation.

There are many different types of relationships that create children, and many different reasons for those relationships to end. For example, perhaps there never really was a relationship, as the child was born out of an encounter that did not develop into something committed and long-term. In that case, co-parenting should be discussed as soon as the parties realize they're going to become parents and are not going to be together romantically.

In the case of romantic relationships that do exist and are ending—whether they are official marriages or not—co-parenting should be discussed at the initial dissolution of the relationship. If you have reached the point where it is certain or even seriously likely that the romantic element of the relationship is ending, that is the time when you need to talk about the details of your new co-parenting relationship.

Today's court system is still affected by the COVID-19 pandemic, which means that there are very long delays in virtually all courts. It takes quite a bit of time to get into a courtroom and to get your case heard, and even longer to get contested matters handled and resolved by a judge or jury.

Therefore, co-parents can be encouraged to essentially take matters into their own hands to work together and create agreements, so long as all parties agree to a foundation of mutual respect and positive communication. Before getting to the point where a court hearing is even possible—which may be long in the future—co-parents can get ahead and figure out together some necessary components of an agreement to best raise their children. After court, it is the co-parents, and not the legal professionals, who will be left to live with the parenting plan in place, and allowing the parties to be involved throughout that process is key to the long-term success.

For example, some of the discussions between co-parents should include what is most important to each party, or what is each side's "non-negotiables". You can also identify the areas in which there is already an agreement. Making lists, taking notes, and re-evaluating priorities will also help the legal professionals be more efficient with your case and finances. Having these issues established and handled will also help you streamline your case in the court system. Streamlining your case this way may even get you in front of a judge a little bit faster, since there are far fewer steps to even a partially resolved case than a completely unresolved case.

From the moment you realize that you are not going to be parenting your children together in one home, it is very important to start talking about co-parenting and what your co-parenting relationship will look like. Discussing co-parenting before the dissolution is finalized helps establish expectations, set guidelines, and ensure a smoother transition for the children. Addressing these matters proactively can contribute to a collaborative co-parenting relationship post-dissolution.

If you are unable to have any fruitful conversations with your co-parent, then working with a professional, like a therapist, parenting facilitator, or attorney, can help you develop your side of the proposed parenting plan. In the end, what you cannot agree to with the other side, can still be succinctly and efficiently presented in the courtroom. Identifying the key areas of concern that will negatively impact a child's best interest early on will ensure the focus remains on the child's welfare. By addressing these concerns, parties can work towards a resolution that prioritizes the child's needs, potentially leading to a more amicable agreement and reducing conflict.

CHAPTER 4

COMMON ISSUES LIKELY TO ARISE IN ALL CO-PARENTING SITUATIONS

The most common issue that I see is fighting over who is going to be the child or children's "primary managing conservator." In Texas, being named a child's primary managing conservator means that conservator may have slightly more control over the child and over decisions related to the child, primarily with respect to residence and school choices.

The primary conservator generally decides where the child or children live (meaning the child or children's primary residence). This often determines where the child or children will go to school, which may be another decision made exclusively by the primary conservator. While primary conservators may also have more time with the children than the other parent, this is not always the case.

Notably, it is possible to avoid naming either party as the primary managing conservator all together. This popular new trend in family law courts allows for a more flexible and balanced approach where both co-parents share decision-making responsibilities and parenting time. Conflict around this issue only arises when one or both parties are committed to the idea of having one primary conservator. In this circumstance, it is important for the legal professionals involved to educate the co-parents on the benefits of avoiding a primary managing conservator and sharing the responsibilities for the children jointly. By avoiding the designation of one parent as the primary managing conservator, it may mitigate potential conflicts or power struggles between the parents, fostering a more cooperative co-parenting relationship.

In these situations, my goal is to help the parties reach an agreement that is better for the child, where perhaps we don't have a single primary conservator. There are tools we can use in situations like this, such as restricting the child's residence to a specific geographical area (regardless of which parent the child lives with for what percentage of the time). We also encourage co-parents to have the child or children continue attending school in one school system for the duration of their education, for the sake of continuity. Because of how public schools are usually organized, the school system often corresponds to the fixed address of the child. Crafting specific geographical restrictions for each family can avoid the pitfalls of a single managing conservator, but also protect the benefits as well. In this environment, both co-parents are now encouraged to work together and cooperate in the best interests of their children, promoting a healthier family dynamic that respects the diverse nature of the modern family.

The second most common source of conflict that we see in co-parents comes down to the amount of time each parent is allotted with the child or children. There is certainly a very strong, very common feeling among parents or caretakers that they feel better about their role as a parent if they think that they have more actual hours in the year with their child than the opposing party. This turns things into a competition which can become very counterproductive.

To combat these conflicts, I always remind the parties that it's not about the number of days or the number of nights they have with the child. Of course, quantity of time is important, and children need to spend a significant quantity of time with their parents to develop a bond and a relationship. But immediately behind the quantity of time is the more important issue of <u>quality of time</u>.

We try to explain to co-parents that it doesn't really matter if you have more hours with the child if that time doesn't amount to quality time. That is, for example, if the majority of a parent's hours take place when the child is in school, or when the parent is working or exhausted from work or otherwise distracted, that isn't really quality time (while it may be a larger quantity of time).

To avoid this co-parenting conflict, our goal is to create parenting plans that allow parents to have quality time with their children, setting aside who has the greater number of hours in a year with their child.

These two issues—the misconception that there has to be one primary conservator/the ensuing conflict about who that will be, and prioritizing quantity of time over quality of time—definitely tend to cause the most disruption to co-parents when trying to create a parenting plan that they can both agree to follow.

When A Co-Parenting Situation Breaks Down, Is There Usually One Parent Who Is Causing The Problems, Or Is It More Common For Both Parents To Be Partially Responsible?

This may be surprising, but I think that more often than not, both parents are at least partially responsible. I think most parents would disagree with that statement, especially if they have particularly difficult co-parents. And of course, there are situations in which one parent is clearly the antagonist and obviously most at fault for derailing the co-parenting relationship.

However, in my experience, when you dive in a little bit deeper and start asking some questions about the thoughts, feelings, past history, and current dynamic of both parties, things look a little less black-and-white most of the time. More often than not, both parties have at least some role in not being able to have a successful co-parenting relationship. By encouraging all of the parties involved to shift their focus from "what is best for me?" to "what is best for our child?" we see much greater successful case closures.

A successful co-parent exercises emotional maturity by: (1) leaving some things left unsaid for the best interest of your child, (2) focusing on how to best serve your child in co-parenting, not just today but five or even ten years from now, and (3) considering the end goal by asking what your child will reflect on this environment in twenty years from now and how you have affected their future decisions. It is important to remember that it is not this moment, the present, that has the most impact. You should focus instead on what the end game is, and what kind of adult will your child be based on these experiences.

As parents, we influence the lenses through which our children view the world. We also have a tremendous responsibility in encouraging and guiding them in ways to be contributing members of our society. If the expectations we create for them, or the reactions we teach to them, have a negative impact on either of these then we are failing. This transitions into co-parenting by remembering that we model relationship behaviors, appropriate boundaries, and controlled reactions throughout that dynamic as well.

CHAPTER 5

BASIC COMPONENTS THAT MAKE UP A POSITIVE, HEALTHY CO-PARENTING RELATIONSHIP

A positive co-parenting relationship starts with:

a) Caregivers who are regulated, strong and healthy independently;
b) Caregivers who are respectful and trusting of the other co-parent;
c) Caregivers who are willing to put what's best for the children first; and

d) Caregivers committed to improving or protecting the co-parenting foundation that they have created so far.

What do I mean by “regulated”? When caregivers and children experience stress, the body activates its natural stress-response systems. These systems cause emotional and physical changes in a person. For example, a caregiver under significant stress may exhibit frustration, irritation, sensitivity and anxiousness. We consider this stress response to be a dysregulated state. Many individuals can go through the regulated and dysregulated cycle several times a day. The return to the regulated state – emotional calmness – in a quick timeframe is the key.

Another key essential element in a good co-parenting relationship is reciprocal trust that the child or children will be provided with good care and support. It is our job and our goal to do everything that we can to build up that trust. If there’s already a break in that trust, or a lack of trust to begin with, then something needs to be done to address it. Regulated caregivers that can offer trust to one another is the strongest foundation for building a co-parenting relationship.

Sometimes, that means that it may be necessary to pursue counseling or therapy. Sometimes there are other remedies. There may need to be limitations and court orders to outline a relationship that allows for the management of unsafe or inappropriate conditions so that trust can flourish in other areas. Whatever method is used, it is essential to instate or re-instate that trust for any successful co-parenting relationship.

Finally, the co-parents need to be focused on building the best possible environment for the child or children. Co-parents need to make sure that their priority is building a co-parenting environment in which the children can thrive, be successful, and be balanced.

My use of the word "thrive" in the above context is deliberate. If they want to establish a truly healthy and successful co-parenting relationship, the priority of the co-parents must be creating an environment in which the child or children can truly thrive, rather than simply cope, accept their new reality, or survive.

Without these foundations established and fully embraced by both parties (both "I've got to respect and trust my co-parent" and "I've got to make sure that I can create an environment where my child can thrive"), there can be no successful co-parenting relationship.

What Are Reasonable Expectations You Should Have For Your Co-Parenting Relationship?

First, you should expect that you will need to compromise at some point. Every co-parent needs to accept a little bit of give-and-take. You're not going to create a parenting plan with your co-parent that gives you a 100% of what your dream parenting plan may have been. This has been true in every single co-parenting case I have ever worked on.

Often, co-parents approach a co-parenting planning situation with "non-negotiables." When I say "non-negotiables", I mean things on which you're not willing to change your mind. These are big issues that you consider lines in the sand, so to speak. These are the things you have decided will not be open for discussion in your parenting plans.

In some cases, "non-negotiables" are reasonable and can remain intact. However, in others, one or both co-parents may find themselves needing to be more flexible about these issues, not to mention being more flexible about other, less-important issues. The less open co-parents are to compromising, the more likely it is for the process to reach an impasse early on.

If you do reach an impasse early on in the case, you will most likely have to abandon the out-of-court negotiation process and go before a judge. To be clear and completely frank, I think every court in Texas would agree that when the judge decides in co-parenting matters, nobody wins. The judge isn't going to give either parent 100% of what they want. The judge is simply going to arbitrate and force the compromise that the co-parents refused to make outside of court. If you enter the mediation or facilitation process open to compromise, however, you can remain much more in control of the final decision, and are much more likely to wind up with more of what you want, rather than less.

It behooves co-parents to remember that once the judge orders a parenting plan, both co-parents will be forced to live with that co-parenting plan. It is difficult to get modifications to these orders, and—if it is even possible to get a modification in your case—it will cost you even more time, money, and stress.

In summary, if you refuse to compromise and force your family's legal case into court, nobody wins. Instead, both co-parents should approach the process from the outset with open-mindedness and flexibility. You can and should identify which points are most important to you, and what you need to discuss with your co-parent. You can and should negotiate on issues that you feel need to be negotiated. However, you have to be willing to meet the other person where they are, within reason.

CHAPTER 6

DO I HAVE TO LIKE MY CHILD'S OTHER PARENT? DO WE HAVE TO BE FRIENDS IN ORDER TO PROVIDE THE STABILITY THAT OUR CHILD NEEDS?

This is always somewhat of a loaded question. Obviously, something occurred in your relationship with your co-parent that caused the end of your romantic relationship (or that caused that relationship not to exist in the first place). Similarly, something happened to make it so that you do not feel comfortable living in the same home as your co-parent, whether or not you are in a romantic relationship. These are perfectly valid, normal, and common occurrences, but they do often color how people relate to one another.

In some cases, co-parents can remain close friends and continue being very affectionate to one another, even loving one another, after their romantic/sexual relationship ends. However, the end of a romantic relationship often complicates and sometimes prohibits those types of interactions and feelings, and that is just as valid.

There's nothing that says that you and your co-parent have to be best friends. Does it happen? Sometimes, sure. But it's certainly not a requirement to have a successful co-parenting relationship.

What is required for a successful co-parenting relationship is mutual respect and trust. That is the level of closeness that has to be maintained so as to not undermine one another or the co-parenting relationship. Instead of holding yourself to the standard of having to like or even be best friends with your co-parent, you simply need to maintain trust and respect. If anything beyond that doesn't feel right, then it isn't necessary.

You also have to "like" the parenting plan that the two of you create together and ultimately agree upon. That is, you have to be able to live a life that is as close as possible to happiness for you within the parameters of the plan. So, if the parenting plan you're working out looks like it's going to require too much (or too little) "friend" time between the co-parents, you need to address that during the planning process. Remember, this is about finding the most sustainable plan that is in the best interest of your children. You have to be able to live with the plan without becoming overly stressed or miserable.

In terms of behavior toward one another, while it is not necessary to actively "like" your co-parent, there is some degree of friendliness and civility that is required. You want to remember this when you interact with them in order to facilitate a healthy co-parenting relationship. Your child is always watching the interactions between his caregivers and making determinations about human relationships based on these observations. Communication is largely non-verbal as well, and so the relationship between the co-parents extends beyond just what they say to each other.

In co-parenting interactions, you want to be treated (and to treat your co-parent) with the same common courtesies and approachability that you receive in any other interactions, whether that's in your personal life, your professional life, or on the street in public.

Does treating everyone with a basic degree of civility mean that mean that you're going to be best friends with everyone you meet? Does treating someone with respect when you interact with them mean that you're going to go get lunch together or pedicures after work one day? No, that's not what I mean by friendliness.

What I mean when I talk about maintaining civility or "friendliness" with your co-parent is that you have to approach the relationship willing to work with that co-parent and to communicate as clearly as possible with them. That includes not being nasty to one another or cutting off communication, and rather, fostering a fundamental promise that you will always be able to communicate important details to one another about your child's care and wellbeing.

In these cases, the baseline of communication that needs to be maintained would fall under the umbrella of, "I will treat this person with friendliness and respect, the same as I would treat a colleague or a person I encountered on the street."

CHAPTER 7

KEY AREAS OF AGREEMENT IN ANY CO-PARENTING RELATIONSHIP

There are several points of agreement that are very important for co-parents to reach or at least attempt to reach.

For example, co-parents should agree on one set of expectations for the child (assuming those expectations are realistic and solely in the child's best interest), as well as a clear set of consequences for the child if they do not meet those expectations. These standards or expectations, as well as consequences, should not vary between homes. They must be consistent if they are to be successful. Children benefit from consistency and the continuity that comes from operating under one set of expectations. Focus on creating a list of agreed acceptable behaviors, unacceptable behaviors, and consequences for that unacceptable behavior. When the majority of consistent behavior expectations and consequences are similar between two homes, the child can learn to thrive in both environments.

Additionally, whenever possible, there should be a single set of moral obligations or expectations for the child that is shared between the two homes. It is very confusing and difficult for a child to process if there are different moral codes to live by in each home.

These expectations might be rooted in religion, or might just be rooted in a strong personal sense of social commitment to humanity. Whether the morality has a strictly religious base or not isn't really important: the issue is how it affects the way the child is taught to treat people.

That is, we don't want to teach a child that in this home, we treat human beings like X, and in that home, we treat human beings like Y. We don't want them to have to follow one moral code this weekend, and another moral code next weekend. It is very difficult for children to learn, comprehend, absorb, and take seriously two completely different sets of expectations or guidelines for basic morality. It can become a battle for children from a very early onset if they get two different moral realities in two different homes. They will be severely conflicted and confused about what is right and what is not.

In application, this means different things in different situations. Does it mean that you have to agree on attending the same church on Sundays? Not necessarily. Does it mean that you have to agree that time out is going to be 10 minutes in each home? This is helpful, but also not necessarily required.

What I'm talking about has more to do with those core fundamental beliefs of what makes a good person in our family. Those beliefs ought to be shared between co-parents.

I also believe that it's very important that there be an agreement about whether or not corporal punishment or corporal discipline is going to be used. Oftentimes, a disagreement about corporal punishment leads to physical discipline in one home and none in another. This creates the space for lots of future litigation as to whether or not that discipline was or is appropriate or excessive. Instead, there should be an agreement about whether or not corporal punishment is on the table. Either it's allowed in both homes, or it's allowed in neither home. This makes for a much smoother transition for the child in-between the two homes.

Consistency in routines and a united front on major decisions contribute to a sense of security for the child. Focusing on the child's happiness and development demonstrates a commitment to the child's best interest and a shared goal of providing your child with a nurturing and loving environment, despite the changes in the family dynamics.

CHAPTER 8

COMPONENTS OF A CO-PARENTING ARRANGEMENT THAT MIGHT BE LESS IMPORTANT TO DIG YOUR FEET IN ON

As a co-parent, it is tremendously important to trust your fellow co-parent. You must be able to trust the co-parent to feed the children a well-balanced meal, to get the child to bed on time, to make sure that they have baths when needed, that they're wearing appropriate clothing to school, and other key caretaking issues.

If you have concerns about your co-parent's ability to do any of those things, that's a much larger issue that you will likely need to address through court orders before creating any sort of healthy co-parenting relationship.

However, if you and your co-parent are both going to be managing conservators (sharing joint custody), and you're both going to be responsible for the raising of your children, then this bottom line of trust that the other co-parent will meet the needs of your children should allow for variation.

Furthermore, micro-managing the other parent's home and childcare is unnecessary in a successful co-parenting relationship. Unless there's a specific reason why we need to insist on it, we wouldn't include something like exactly when dinner is served each night. Or, for instance, what exactly needs to be served for dinner at the other parent's home. If there is a basis of trust that the children will be cared for, co-parents should not introduce micromanagement into the parenting plan.

Parenting plans are for broader issues. They are not for issues like which days of the week the child gets a bath, or how long the bath should be, or what time the child has to get up in the morning on weekends and weekdays. If the child's needs are being met and they are kept healthy and happy, co-parents are not serving the process by digging their heels in on these issues.

For these kinds of things, parents are going to have to extend enough trust to their co-parent to make good decisions for their child. It can be difficult to learn this, but it is essential that both parents understand that there are things that they are not going to be able to dictate in their co-parent's home.

I find that this level of trust and lack of control is hardest to extend for whichever co-parent has had the most control over the day-to-day care of the child before the divorce or separation. While we can appreciate that it will be hard for that parent to let those smaller things go, because they have had such a large degree of control over—and responsibility for—

these decisions for so long, preserving the promise of a successful co-parenting relationship requires it.

Though it may be difficult, both parents are going to have to do the work of letting those smaller degrees of control go when they are not having parenting time with their children. In doing so, they will be putting some faith in their co-parent's ability to make those decisions properly and in the best interests of the children involved. In the end, once you know for sure that your co-parent is responsible and acting in good faith, you can trust that they're going to be able to make those decisions to help your child thrive between both homes.

Often times, parents eventually find that they don't have the energy to spend to be concerned about these smaller things, or second-guessing what is being followed and what is not. It is far more useful and beneficial to the child to spend your energy as a parent on creating quality parenting time with your child.

In Your Experience, Are There Components Of A Co-Parenting Relationship That Should Be Totally Off The Table For Discussion Between Co-Parents?

No. I think everything should be open for discussion between co-parents when it comes to components of the co-parenting relationship.

Sometimes that means that an agreement will be reached, and sometimes that means an agreement won't be reached. However, everything should be open for discussion in a healthy and productive, non-judgmental way between the co-parents.

CHAPTER 9

ESSENTIAL RULES TO FOLLOW IN YOUR CO-PARENTING SITUATION

I am often asked about the most essential rules for co-parents to follow. After years of experience, I have managed to narrow it down to a few basic rules that will serve all co-parents.

Perhaps the single most important co-parenting rule to follow is this: always put your child's needs first. Not your needs, not your co-parenting relationship's needs, but your child's needs. If both parties can keep the child's needs at the forefront, they will have the best chance at a successful co-parenting relationship.

Additionally, putting the child's needs first ensures that the child's well-being and emotional stability remain paramount for both parties. This helps to create a supportive environment where open communication is encouraged, ensuring that the child maintains a health relationship with both parents. Co-parenting with empathy and cooperation helps minimize the impact that the separation will have on the child. Ultimately, putting your child's needs first requires ongoing dedication, flexibility, and a shared goal of helping your child thrive in the new environment.

This is the cardinal rule of co-parenting. However, there are a couple of other rules that I think arc important.

- Always Work Together. I think it's important that parents work together to ensure their child's psychological, spiritual, and physical wellbeing, as well as their safety. These needs have to be met for the child in both homes. This rule is something of an accompaniment to putting your child's needs first. Ensure that your child has a smooth transition between each of his homes by working with your co-parent to make each transition easy and expected for the child.

- Always Communicate. Communication is also key to a healthy co-parenting relationship. You should always be communicating with your co-parent about anything of importance to your child. If there has been a change in plans (or if you would like to request one), communication is paramount. The line of communication should always be kept open, and both co-parents should always be kept informed and in-the-loop. The communication should clearly define expectations, schedules, and responsibilities – helping to avoid many future misunderstandings. Using various communication tools such as e-mail, messaging apps, or co-parenting apps can provide a structured platform for discussions.

It is essential that co-parents avoid hiding anything that has to do with the child, or depriving the other parent of information that pertains to how the child is doing when they are away from said parent. It is wildly unproductive to say things like, "This is my time, and you don't need to worry about how he's doing here." That sort of mentality will set you up for failure and resentment outright. Remember to stay focused on the child's needs, keep emotions in check, and compromise. Regular check-ins to discuss important aspects of the child's life can foster cooperation between co-parents and allow for adapting to changing circumstances when necessary.

If you're not willing to communicate with your co-parent, you're certainly not putting your child's needs first. It goes without saying, in my opinion, that both co-parents must be involved in providing for the child's needs. As transitions occur and the child moves between houses, there must be communication between co-parents to ensure continuity between them. This way, they will know what to expect week in and week out, and what might be going on with the child this week because of something that happened last week, when they were at their other parent's house. Furthermore, do not misread this to believe that there cannot be specialized safety measures in place to protect each parent or the child in a particular case. But safety measures needed in your specific case do not obviate the need to remember these few rules. The overarching goal is to create a positive and supportive co-parenting environment through clear, constructive, and child-centered communication.

CHAPTER 10

WHY IS GOOD COMMUNICATION BETWEEN CO-PARENTS SO CRITICAL?

If you don't have good communication with your co-parent, your co-parenting relationship and the wellbeing of your child could be harmed in several ways.

First, it becomes difficult for your child to transition between their two households. Often, if the child is old enough to perceive the lack of communication between their parents, they may feel that it is now their burden to facilitate communication between two resistant adults. We never want to put a child in the middle like that. To avoid getting to that point, we want parents communicating with each other openly and honestly about how the child is doing, so that the child doesn't feel compelled to take on that role. Maintaining open and honest dialogue is crucial. If co-parents aren't communicating well, then the child might not get all of their needs met sufficiently. Both parents should feel comfortable expressing their thoughts, concerns, and ideas. Active listening is equally important, ensuring that each party understands the other's perspective. Communication forms the foundation for a healthy and effective co-parenting relationship.

For example, let's say that the child's teacher sent a note home on one of Parent A's nights saying that the child needs extra reading lessons at home to improve their vocabulary. If Parent A never communicates this to Parent B, then Parent B will not know to give the child extra reading lessons, and the child will miss out on the opportunity to get these lessons every night—simply because Parent A happened to have custody of the child on the night that the teacher sent the note home.

In this scenario, the only one being harmed is the child. Parent B doesn't need the extra reading lessons and will not suffer any harm if the child doesn't catch up on his vocabulary words, for example. So, when parents withhold or neglect communication with their co-parent, it is often the case that the only person suffering is the child. This is why communication is so important: so that we can ensure that the child doesn't suffer from the lack of information being passed between the two parties. In contrast, open communication ensures that both parents are on the same page regarding the child's needs, routines, and development. Communication also helps establish and maintain consistent parenting strategies, rules, and expectations between households.

What About Co-Parents Who Are On Very Tense Or Unfriendly Terms? Are There Methods Of Communication That Are Best To Use In Order To Exchange Information While Avoiding Conflict?

Let's just say first that technology is a wonderful thing. As mentioned earlier, several products have hit the market in the last decade to address the specific communication needs of co-parents with this specific sort of dynamic.

For example, there are several applications that you can put on your phone to help you co-parent, which includes the ability to communicate by text. All communications on the app are independently archived, so neither party can delete them, and both can have a record of what has been said, and when it has been said. The app also includes the ability to share and save relevant files, images, and links, as well as the child's various calendars (school calendars, sports and extracurricular calendars, medical appointment calendars, etc.).

These sorts of apps also allow for the sharing of bills and payments to be made if part of your co-parenting plan includes cost-sharing. They allow for the sharing of schedules, appointment reminders, education notes and much more.

A handful of apps out on the market today assist parents with communicating more efficiently. You can load this information onto your cellphone and have that co-parenting organization and communication right there in one spot, on the device you always carry with you. This streamlines the process, saves time and reduces stress by providing helpful access to essential information even when a parent isn't physically with their child.

If you're not that technologically savvy, or you don't feel comfortable having an app on your phone, a co-parenting journal or a notebook that travels between the homes is also an excellent tool for anti-conflict communication between co-parents.

In these notebooks, parents can write down anything their co-parent needs to know about how the previous week went, as well as anything that might have been communicated by the school, or any other piece of pertinent information. You can also print out and include the child's schedule for school, extracurricular activities, and appointments, and tape it to one of the notebook pages.

I think the most important thing when discussing communication is not what type of communication device the family picks, but that both parties agree that they are going to use it, and actually follow through. After all, there's no point in any device or tool if one parent refuses or decides not to use it.

It's actually very common in many courts to order the use of a specific device or tool for communication between co-parents. Usually, co-parents can choose the specific tool or method. However, if they can't reach an agreement, the judge may pick one for them. In any case, as long as both parties agree to use the same tool or application to communicate, then there really is a wide variety of options to choose from.

Creating a healthy communication environment is essential for resolving conflicts that arise between co-parents, as well. When disagreements happen, open dialogue allows co-parents to address issues constructively, find compromises, and prevent disputes from negatively impacting the child. This extends further to the child by helping to alleviate any anxiety or uncertainty the child may feel. It reassures them that both parents are actively involved and engaged with their child.

CHAPTER 11

WHEN COMMUNICATING WITH MY CHILD'S OTHER PARENT, WHAT SHOULD I KEEP IN MIND?

There are certain guidelines to be mindful of when communicating with your co-parent.

As an aside, any family law attorney will remind their client that when communicating with your co-parent in a way that is recordable, or if you are communicating with them in writing, remember that it can be used against you at a later date.

If you say anything abusive, disrespectful, or accusatory, or anything that shows a lack of trust in the other parent, those things can certainly be used against you in court by the other co-parent's counsel or attorney.

Furthermore, we are reminded that our communication is a model of human relationships for our children. They observe tone, facial expressions, word choice, frequency and the energy surrounding the communications. Demonstrating respectful and cooperative communication teaches children valuable interpersonal skills and conflict resolution techniques. This is one of the many reasons why it is important that the co-parents agree on a set of rules for communication or how they're going to address or speak to one another. This can include rules such as:

- Not using foul language;
- Not interrupting;
- Not delivering ultimatums; and
- Not asking the child which home they like better.

The focus of co-parenting communication should be on sharing of information about how the child is doing while in your care, so that the other caregiver knows how to transition the child into their home and vice-versa. Focus on keeping your communication brief, informative, factual, and friendly.

In the end, if your communication remains respectful and focuses on ensuring that all your child's educational, emotional, spiritual, and physical needs are being met in both of the homes, then you don't really need to worry about putting communication rules in place, and you don't really need to worry about what you say being used against you.

As an aside, when we say communication being used against you, we are usually referring to communication in which you are attacking your co-parent. Attacking your co-parent means you are generally not focusing on what's best for your child, which can put you in danger in Court, and can put your child in danger of generally negative outcomes.

You may work with a Parenting Facilitator or Parent Coordinator to practice communication with your co-parent and to craft a set of rules for what written or spoken communication will entail. Creating these boundaries and foundations early will help create a strong, sustainable co-parenting relationship.

We Don't Yet Have The Skill-Set Necessary To Effectively Communicate. How Can We As Parents Communicate More Effectively For The Sake Of Our Kids And Our Own Wellbeing?

For co-parents who are starting from scratch and developing the skills to communicate, I think the most important thing is come up with some guidelines and some rules about how you're going to communicate with one another.

Some parents limit the number of communications (i.e., texts and calls) between co-parents per day. It's also helpful to establish a standard of information that needs to be shared. That is, you don't need to tell your co-parent or ask your co-parent about every single thing the child has done every single minute of the day.

You want to keep communication focused on what your co-parent needs to know. For example, how did the doctor's appointment go today? How was school today? That is the sort of information I need to know now, and that's appropriate to ask. Asking, "why did you decide to do that last week" instead of focusing on present caregiving, does not focus on what the child needs now and keeping that at the forefront.

Be respectful. Maintain a respectful tone in your conversations (written and verbal) with your co-parent. Avoid blame, accusations, or negative language.

Prioritize the child. Keep the focus on the child's well-being and needs. Do not use communication to air your personal grievances or try to get back at your co-parent for some perceived wrongdoing.

Be clear and concise. Using straightforward and concise language to communicate information about your child's schedule, health, and any routine changes will help avoid misunderstandings. It also leaves little room for emotion or backlash.

Establish consistent communication methods. Using the same method and manner for communication will promote streamlined sharing of information.

Set boundaries. This means that you should set limits on frequency and timing of communication. You should also respect your co-parent's time with the child, personal time, and privacy. Ensure that essential information is shared appropriately and timely for the situation.

Share your calendar. Many parent apps allow for a shared calendar for the child's events. This is important. You can use this shared calendar for the child's activities, appointments, and important dates. This helps the whole family to plan accordingly.

Be flexible. Acknowledge that unexpected situations will arise. Everything will NOT go according to plan all the time! Be open to adjusting schedules or plans when necessary and communicate these changes promptly.

Know what to do in an emergency. Both caregivers should agree early on how information will be shared in an emergency. Important contact information for doctors, schools, and emergency contacts should be shared between both caregivers.

Use appropriate names. Refer to the co-parent respectfully by their name, and refrain, for example, from calling your co-parent things like "my child's sperm donor." Unfortunately, that's a common phrase we hear, especially if there's acrimony between the co-parents. Remain polite and respectful, using words like please and thank you, or asking things like, "Do you mind sharing with me?"

Many of these guidelines are the sort of basic communication skills that we learn as young children, but which often get left behind during divorce or separation. Let's not forget them.

How Do I Work With And Come To An Agreement With A Co-Parent Who Is Geared More Toward Conflict And Fighting?

I always tell my clients that two wrongs don't make a right. If you're dealing with a co-parent who insists on doing wrong (i.e., trying to stir up conflict and fights), the best move on your part is to try to redirect and focus all communication to what is important for your child's wellbeing.

Attempts to start conflicts are rather easy to spot, especially if this is someone you know very well (such as an ex-spouse). Redirect those false starts into conversations about things that are necessary to make sure your child is thriving between your two homes.

If your co-parent insists on talking about your communication style or your interpersonal interactions, simply remain calm, refuse to take the bait, and redirect the conversation to how you can both ensure that the way you relate to each other is in the best interest of your child. If conversations become hostile, communicate your willingness to discuss matters civilly and suggest taking a break in communication when needed.

Ensure that you do not place blame. If you focus on using "I" statements, and express your feelings without sounding accusatory, you can shift your focus away from the problem and towards finding the solution. This is always more productive.

It is my experience that in most cases, if you continue to redirect and steer conversations in that direction over time, if you remain unresponsive to any attacks or goading and do not feel the need to defend yourself (since any allegations are designed to cause conflict), communication with your co-parent will improve and become more cooperative.

If someone is attacking you or if you feel attacked, it's understandable that your first impulse is to feel defensive. That's perfectly natural. However, for the sake of your co-parenting relationship, you must resist the urge to act on that impulse. When co-parents get defensive, they tend to get angry, and that's when communication begins to break down. So, sometimes, the best option is to simply ignore. And know when to disengage. If a conversation is becoming too heated, recognize when it's time to disengage temporarily. You can always revisit the discussion later when emotions have subsided.

Is It Okay To Set Limits With My Co-Parent When It Comes To How They Handle Certain Things Related To Our Child? What Are Reasonable And Unreasonable Limits?

Yes, it is acceptable to set limits and boundaries with a co-parent.

In every co-parenting relationship, there are certain things that are agreed upon by both parties. These can be considered "limits" of a sort. Insist on respectful and civil communication. Set a limit on name-calling, insults, or any form of verbal abuse.

You may also want to create family rules and discipline agreements for your child to help show stability and emotional consistency. You will want to insure that both parents emphasize the importance of adhering to the parenting schedule and encourage the child to enjoy time with both parents. Consistency and support helps your child feel secure. Limit or stop any attempts by a caregiver to bad mouth or discourage the child's time with their other parent.

It's essential to be in continual communication with your co-parent about these guidelines or limits for how you have agreed to construct an environment for your child. Co-parents should be regularly checking in to make sure that they're communicating and that they're still on the same page about those limits, and that one party's perspective on the situation hasn't changed. And remember, if you are setting a limit for your co-parent, you should also be prepared to follow and respect that limit.

Chapter 12

What if My Co-Parent Refuses to Listen or Be Respectful, Even When We're Trying to Make Decisions Or Resolve Conflicts?

This can be a very difficult situation to deal with. However, it is not insurmountable. Often, the most important thing is to express your concerns calmly and clearly by encouraging open dialogue and cooperation.

It is essential to approach these relationships with patience and a focus on finding solutions. You may need to take a step back and give certain situations a moment to calm down. All you want to prioritize is your child's well-being. You do not have to be right or owed anything if the child is the focus (and not you). Cooperation may take time, and persistence in seeking constructive solutions is key.

Many times we feel pressure to make decisions or resolve conflicts immediately, which raises the stakes and makes it more likely for parents who are prone to conflict and defensiveness to get, well, confrontational and defensive. Sometimes in response, even the less confrontational and defensive parent becomes frustrated and tries to push the issue right that moment.

Instead, I think it's essential to see the good that can come from realizing that sometimes a decision or resolution doesn't get made exactly when you want it to.

If things are getting heated, the best thing to do is often to take a step back and allow the heat of the moment to dissipate. Then, you can re-approach, either on a different day or a different time. Sometimes, you can even shift communication mediums to great effect: in certain cases, just creating the separation or barrier of not being face-to-face (i.e., communicating on the phone, by text, by email, or in writing, perhaps by using one of the apps that we've talked about or by writing something in the co-parenting notebook) can be very helpful.

If your co-parent continues to be blatantly disrespectful, or refuses to listen to what you're saying, then at some point you may need to reach out for help. This is the point at which a co-parenting counselor, coordinator, therapist, or parenting facilitator can be enlisted to work with your co-parent. Ideally, they will help your co-parent understand why the level of disrespect, distrust, and basic lack of manners in their communication is impeding their child's ability to thrive between the two homes, and why it is so important to prevent that.

Avoid the kneejerk reaction of going to the court first. Therapists, coordinators, and parenting facilitators are far better suited than the court to explain why communication needs to be respectful for the benefit of the child.

If you are struggling with a persistently incommunicative or disrespectful co-parent, I would strongly urge you to consider bringing in a professional to help build a strong co-parenting foundation before going to the court.

CHAPTER 13

WHY IS IT BEST TO STAY OUT OF THE COURTROOM IF POSSIBLE?

Staying out of the courtroom is and should be one of the primary goals of co-parents. Every family court judge in the country would probably tell you that when you come into the courtroom in these cases, nobody wins. Everybody loses some aspect of what they came in looking for that day.

Cost should be a strong factor in considering court involvement. Legal proceedings can be expensive, both financially and emotionally. The lengthy, and time-consuming process creates extra stress and emotional strain for the co-parents and the children involved. In addition, you almost always wind up with a stranger making essential, life-changing decisions for both you and your child. Nobody knows your child and your child's needs like you and your co-parent do. You and your co-parent are the two most equipped people to make decisions for your child, and to understand their needs and what's important for them to be able to thrive in their two homes.

If you can't work with your co-parent because they are disrespectful or they are unwilling to communicate or won't accept some of your limits or vice versa, then that's when it's time to involve a professional—and we highly recommend first attempting to work with a parenting facilitator or counselor.

Parenting facilitation is particularly useful in these cases, as parent facilitators are specifically trained in working with each co-parent individually so that they understand that the first and primary focus of a co-parenting relationship is making sure the child's needs are being put first. Parenting facilitators are also adept at making sure that both co-parents understand that the ultimate goal here is to help the child thrive, not just survive, in the environment that the co-parents are creating together.

If a parenting facilitator can help work with both co-parents to establish that foundation, then the co-parents can start to work together with the parenting facilitator to come up with parenting plans that both parties can accept. Ultimately, the goal is to create an environment that both parties can agree to support and maintain to help the child thrive.

If you already have a divorce or custody attorney—someone who is helping you dissolve a marriage or create the initial draft of a co-parenting plan or a custody agreement—you will want to reach back out to that attorney and ask them how to get a parenting facilitator involved, as well as how can we compel the other co-parent to attend parenting facilitation.

Importantly, this is the sort of thing that won't work unless both parents are ready, willing, and able to fully participate. If one parent is resisting, then at that point it might be necessary to go to the court, simply to ask for an order that both parents attend some sort of parenting facilitation or some co-parenting education.

Successful parenting agreements come from these facilitation sessions and from earnest engagement with parenting education, not from arbitrations of the court.

Additionally, when co-parents lose sight of what is best for the child, an Amicus Attorney can help re-focus the parties on meeting the child's needs first. An Amicus Attorney looks at all the details of the case and takes extensive interviews in order to write a report to the court about what they think is best for the child. Amicus Attorneys are helpful because they can serve as a neutral third party who is able to determine what is best for the child, without getting bogged down in disagreement between the parties.

In addition, it also may be necessary for everyone involved to participate in some sort of therapy or counseling. A therapist can help safely voice, explore, and work through the processing of feelings associated with the separation of the family unit, such as heartbreak or a sense of betrayal, or anything else people may be feeling. This process helps people move forward, and to make great strides toward building a successful co-parenting foundation. Once this foundation is established, it provides the basis for a long-term, healthy, and successful co-parenting relationship.

What Is Your Best Advice To Co-Parents Who Are Struggling In Their Current Arrangements? What Is Your Best Advice For Co-Parents Who Are Just Starting The Process Of Developing A Co-Parent Relationship, And Are Worried About What Could Happen?

Your first step in evaluating your current parenting situation is self-reflection. You should ask yourself what is most important to you in a co-parenting relationship—or rather, what will best enable you to create an environment for your child in which they can thrive. What does that look like in your household? What do you need from your co-parent to facilitate that reality?

Once you have that framework established, you have a foundation from which you can approach your co-parent. You will be able to match up your values and anticipate which things will be easier to agree upon and which things will be harder.

If you reach an impasse, or even several impasses, on issues that are disagreements between co-parents, it may become necessary to involve a third-party mediator, such as a parenting facilitator or a co-parenting counselor, to help you resolve these issues.

Usually, the resolution a professional of this sort will help you come to is that either there will not be an agreement on this issue and it's not as important as you initially thought it was, or that there must be an agreement on this issue, and you are going to find a way toward an agreement together.

In the end, again, all of this does not work unless the focus is on making sure the child is doing the best he possibly can in this environment.

So, to re-iterate: start with some self-reflection, and then make sure that you can whittle down your wants and needs to the bare-minimum as a foundation to approach your co-parent. Then, compare and contrast your respective bare minimums. If there are things that you can't reach an agreement on that are very important to you and very important to the success of the co-parenting relationship (and therefore the best interests of the child), you can use the help of a professional to either re-focus your priorities and drop it or come to some sort of mutually agreeable resolution with your co-parent.

In conclusion, work towards building a successful co-parenting relationship by stopping the fighting and start communicating. Recognize the obstacles that exist in your family preventing your child from thriving between both homes and be flexible on how to resolve those obstacles. It is important to remember that this often means employing an alternative to the courtroom battle. Identify your child's needs and create a co-parenting plan that meets those needs without sacrificing a child's relationship with his caregivers. Your child will thank you!

What Is The Next Step?

The next steps in your co-parenting journey could involve ongoing efforts to improve communication, collaborate more effectively, and foster understanding between co-parents. Continue to refine your communication strategies. Focus on clarity, respect, and child-centered interactions.

Work towards the enhanced shared decision-making processes. Both parents should be involved in important choices regarding the child's education, health, and other key aspects. This will also include flexibility and adaptability as your child's needs change and evolve. When necessary, you may need to involve a professional to ensure your child's emotional well-being is monitored and supported.

Co-parenting is an ongoing process that requires commitment and effort from both parties. Continuously seeking ways to improve communication, understanding and a positive environment for your child's growth and development.

INDEX

R

S

T

U

NOTES

Made in the USA
Monee, IL
05 November 2026

67387970R00062